A Little Book on Business Law

Business Structures

Mark Bolton

Copyright © 2020 Mark Bolton

Phone: 0424 425 050

Email: mark@boltonlegal.com.au

Level 2, 21 View Point, Bendigo

PO Box 395, Bendigo, VIC 3552

Photography by Grace Bolton

All rights reserved.

ISBN: 9798664927993

Imprint: Independently published

Dedication

This book is dedicated to my four wonderful children, Ben, Zara, Grace and Maeve.

Thank you

I would like to take this opportunity to say a huge thank you to the following people who have helped me get this little book off the ground:

Penny Bolton,

John Bolton (Dad),

Lauren Bolton,

Natalie Claughton, and

Jenny Delaney.

I would like to make a special mention to barrister and author, Peter Agardy, whose feedback and encouragement have been invaluable, and his books inspirational.

A bit about me

I am a Law Institute of Victoria Accredited Specialist in Commercial Law.

Since 2016 I have run my own practice in the heart of Bendigo, dedicated to helping regional Victorian businesses. For more information about my law practice, go to – www.boltonlegal.com.au.

As well as running my practice, I also teach business law at La Trobe University.

My other passion is writing. I have worked as an inhouse and freelance writer for various business-related publications. Over the years I have written an odd assortment of quirky fiction, children's books, and plays.

Disclaimer

As a lawyer, I cannot help but put in my little disclaimer. This book is supposed to be helpful, but it is general in nature and should not be considered as advice.

Also, the laws that are considered are complicated and constantly changing. This book is not intended to provide an account of the laws, rather to help you understand how it all works.

It is my hope that, rather than provide you with the answers you need, to instead leave you with an understanding that empowers you to ask the right questions.

Contents

PART 1 UNDERSTANDING	14
Different entity types	15
Sole traders	17
Partnerships	24
Companies	35
Different structure types	57
Trusts	59
Combination structures	80
Other common business arrangements	93
PART 2 IDENTIFICATION	98
Business identifiers	99
How to identify another business	109
References	118

When you were 10

Before you get stuck into this book, I want you to go and get out your old grade 5 school photo and try and remember what it was like. I am not talking about your superficial memories of playing tiggy in the glorious autumn sunshine. I am talking about the real memories. I am talking about the never-ending struggle to form alliances, avoid bullies and protect your lunch. I am talking about the time when Ernie Duncan tried to steal your new pencil case but instead you politely explained to him that it was actually your older brother's pencil case and that if he did not give it back your older brother was probably going find Ernie and get it back, together with a few of Ernie's teeth for good measure, and how Ernie graciously returned your pencil case and left you alone.

It is that survival mindset you had as a ten-year-old navigating the schoolyard that I need you to remember and adopt as your read through this book, because business structuring is all about protecting yourself in the face of an uncompromising and sometimes-cruel business world.

Take for example the practice of wealthy individuals putting their homes in the names of their spouse. This is not because they particularly love their spouse, rather it is to make sure that if they get into financial trouble, regardless of all the people they owe money to, they get to keep their home.

Then there are companies, which are primarily used to separate the debts and liabilities of the business from its owners, so that if the business goes bust, the owners avoid responsibility.

You can also take companies a step further and consider the law that requires a director to always act in the best interests of the company. If you think about it, this is effectively a legal requirement for directors and companies to look after themselves, often to the detriment of others.

Then we have trusts, which are these days often used in business mainly to protect personal assets and to minimise tax.

These are just a few of many arrangements and practices that are commonly used to look after *numero uno*. What is relevant is that all these practices are done without any moral or social consideration whatsoever – they are expected of a sophisticated business owner.

The point is that as a business owner, you cannot sit back and hope that other businesses will be nice and reasonable, instead you have to expect and prepare for every business you deal with to have measures in place to make sure that if there is an issue between the two of you, they will automatically come out on top, or at the least unscathed.

A lot of what this book is about is helping you understand how different entities and structures work so that you can use this information to set up your own protection.

It is also so you can understand what protection others have in place so that when you go into transactions and dealings, it is with your eyes open.

At the end of the day, it will be up to you to decide what you do, but when it comes to business structuring, it really is, better the devil you know than the devil you don't.

That leads me onto another reason I want you to remember what it was like when you were 10 – curiosity. When you were 10 you desperately wanted to find out how things worked, all those little secrets about the world that adults seemed to guard so carefully.

As we get older, we seem to lose that curiosity and desire to understand, and topics like business structures get thrown into the too hard / cannot be bothered basket.

It is my hope that this little book will provide the secret into what wealthy and sophisticated business owners do to protect themselves and to pay less tax.

Come on, stop stuffing around on your Game Boy and let's get cracking.

The format of this book

Part 1 on the book is about understanding the different business structures.

We start by looking at the different entity types – **sole traders**, **partnerships** and **companies**. After you understand how the different entity types work, we then move on to structures, being **trusts** and **combination structures**.

For each of the options we look at:

- what they are,
- how they work,
- how they are set up,
- how they are taxed,
- what are their pros and cons, and
- when to use them.

I also give a rating out of five for each of the key features to consider when looking at the different options:

1. **Cost**, being the cost of setting up and ongoing running costs.
2. **Ease**, being the ease of setting up and operating.
3. **Asset protection**, whether your personal assets are protected.
4. **Tax minimisation**, whether there is flexibility to allow for income to be distributed to those on a lower tax bracket, so you pay less tax.
5. **Flexibility**, whether you can easily add or remove owners as the business evolves.

In keeping with the 'When you were 10' theme, and as a little bit of a joke, I start each section with an explanation I would give if I was explaining the concepts to myself when I was 10.

Once you have your head around the different entities and structures, I quickly touch on a couple of other common business arrangements, **joint ventures** and **franchises**.

Part 2 of the book is about identifying businesses and their structures.

To do this we start by looking at the different business identifiers, Australian Business Numbers (*ABN*), Business names, Australian Company Numbers (*ACN*) and verification of identity.

To finish off, we have a three-step process and checklist to work through when you want to identify a business, such as a new customer.

Ernie Duncan

Now let us get back to when you were 10 and that snotty-nosed kid, Ernie Duncan tried to steal your pencil case. Well, it turns out that Ernie has become a successful business owner and he wants to be your first customer.

Ernie tells you he is going to be your best customer and he starts by putting in a big order. Of course Ernie does not have cash to pay upfront, instead he wants you to set up a credit account for his business.

Ernie's business is run through his company, Ernie Pty Ltd.

Ernie is the sole director and sole shareholder of Ernie Pty Ltd.

But it does not stop there...

Ernie Pty Ltd is operating as the trustee of his unit trust, The Ernie Unit Trust.

All the units in The Ernie Unit Trust are owned by Ernie.

Again, it keeps going...

Ernie owns the units in his capacity as trustee of his discretionary trust, The Ernie Family Trust.

The beneficiaries of The Ernie Family Trust include Ernie, Ernie's wife, his kids and all the rest of his extended family.

By the end of this book, you should be able to understand what Ernie's arrangement means and what impact it will have when Ernie fails to pay the money he owes you and you want to sue to get it back.

PART 1
UNDERSTANDING

Different entity types

When you enter into a contract with another business, the first thing you need to work out is the **entity** you are dealing with.

There are three main types of entities used in business: sole trader, partnership and company. It is the entity who will be entering into the contract on behalf of the business.

The next step is to find out the **structure** of the business. The structure is the framework and agreed relationships for which the entity operates, which could include a trust. Knowing the structure will help you work out what recourse you have against the assets of the business if the contract goes pear-shaped.

In the case of Ernie Duncan, the **entity** his business is using is a company, Ernie Pty Ltd, so any contract or agreement will need to be executed by that company.

Together with the company, Ernie Pty Ltd, sitting at the top, it is then with the rest of his arrangement that forms the **structure**. In Ernie's case, the structure is:

- Ernie Pty Ltd as trustee for The Ernie Unit Trust with the units held by Ernie as trustee for The Ernie Family Trust.

The reason why Ernie's structure is important is because the different layers are used to put barriers between you and the assets of the business and Ernie's personal assets.

Do not worry if the above structure does not make sense at this stage.

Sole traders

Explain it to me like I'm a 10-year-old...

A sole trader is the He-Man of the business world.

As you know, He-Man's real name is Prince Adam and it is only when he raises his Power Sword and proclaims, 'by the power of Grayskull... ', does he turn into He-Man. The reality is that He-Man is not much different to Prince Adam. He has a slightly deeper voice and slightly darker skin and hair and a spiffy warrior's outfit, but let us be honest, we all know it is just Prince Adam.

That is effectively the same as a sole trader. Sure, a sole trader can register a new business name and, with his or her Australian Business Number (ABN) in tow, she or he has the power to enter into contracts and employ people, but if things go bad, it will be the individual owner who will be personally responsible.

What is a sole trader?

A sole trader is simply an individual who operates a business as themself.

How does a sole trader work?

As a sole trader it is you personally who is responsible for the business – any contracts entered into are entered into by you personally, any money earned is your personal income and any debts owed are owed by you personally.

Sole traders can transact just like every other business - they can enter into contracts, employ people and lease premises. There is no reason why you could not build a business empire as a sole trader (although I am not personally aware of anyone who has done that).

As the name suggests, however, a sole trader can only be one person. As soon as another person is involved in the ownership of the business, it becomes a partnership.

How to become a sole trader?

To become a sole trader, all you need to do is get an ABN (Australian Business Number). There is a section on ABNs later in the book.

Once you have your ABN, you are good to go.

As a sole trader, you can operate in your own name, or if you want to use a different name, you can operate under a Registered Business Name, also discussed later in the book.

How is a sole trader taxed?

As I mentioned, any profit you earn as a sole trader is simply your own income that you are personally taxed on.

Because you are running your own business, you are able to deduct business expenses from your revenue to calculate your income.

What are the pros and cons of being a sole trader?

The biggest selling features of a sole trader are the cost and ease. All you need to do is register your ABN and you are good to go.

Where a sole trader falls-down is in the two key areas of business structuring – asset protection and tax minimisation.

From an asset protection perspective, basically you have none. If a sole trader gets sued, all his or her business and personal assets are on the chopping block.

In terms of tax minimisation, any income you make is automatically yours, so there is no chance to distribute income to someone in your family on a lower tax bracket.

Finally, as the name suggests, a sole trader can only be one person. As soon as you want to add another person to the ownership of the business you need to consider one of the other entity types – partnership or company.

When to be a sole trader?

If you are going into business by yourself and you do not have much money or assets to protect and just want to get going with things, you might go for the sole trader. On the downside, being sole trader does not give you any protection.

Sole trader rating

Feature	Rating (1 = bad, 5 = good)
Cost	★ ★ ★ ★ ★
Ease	★ ★ ★ ★ ★
Asset protection	★ ★
Tax minimisation	★
Flexibility	★

Partnerships

Explain it to me like I'm a 10-year-old...

A partnership is like Voltron.

As you know, Voltron is an awesome human-shaped robot that is formed when the five robot lions come together. The black lion forms the body, the red and green lions form the arms and the blue and yellow lions form the legs.

Like Voltron, once the individual partners come together, they create a new entity – the partnership.

When Voltron is in action, if something happens to him, regardless of which part of the body gets hurt, it affects all the lions because at that time they are not individuals, they are just a piece of Voltron. This is the same for partnerships. If an individual partner gets in trouble while in the partnership, it affects all the partners together.

What is a partnership?

Most people are familiar with partnerships. Simply, a partnership is a group of two or more people who own and run a business together.

How does a partnership work?

By going into partnership with each other, the partners create what is sometimes called a 'firm'.[1] Each partner then becomes an agent for the firm for the purpose of running the business.[2] As an agent of the firm, each partner can transact on behalf of the firm.[3]

What this means is that each individual partner can do things on behalf of the partnership, such as sign a contract or enter into a lease, and, as long as it is in the ordinary course of business, anything that individual partner does will bind the partnership and the other partners.

The flow-on effect is that if the partnership owes any money, the partners are all personally liable.[4] This also applies if an individual partner does something in the ordinary course of business which causes loss or injury, in which case, again, the partner are all personally liable.[5]

It is important to note that the joint liability and responsibility only applies if a partner is acting in the ordinary course of the partnership's business. A partner is not liable if another partner makes a bad personal investment or does not pay his or her personal tax.

How to set up a partnership?

It is extremely easy to set up a partnership. If you are carrying on a business in common with other people with a view of profit, you will most likely be in a partnership.[6] You do not need to sign anything or register the partnership – you just need to be carrying on the business together. It is as simple as that.

Like all the business types, for tax purposes you will need to get an ABN.

You may want to also register a business name. If you do not register a business name you will need to use all partners' names as the business's name.

With partnerships having been around for so long, there is well established law on how partnerships are to be run.[7] This includes how partnership property and income is to be shared[8] and how a partnership is to be dissolved[9].

There is, however, scope for the partners to agree amongst themselves on how things are to be run.[10] This is usually done in the form of a partnership agreement.

Ending a partnership

Technically, a partnership will automatically come to an end whenever there is a change in the composition of the partnership, this could be an old partner leaving or a new partner joining.[11]

If the partnership is running a business and the remaining partners want to continue the business in partnership, the change in partners is called a technical dissolution the new partnership is considered a reconstituted partnership.[12]

As long as the Australian Taxation Office is notified, the reconstituted partnership can continue to use its existing Tax File Number (TFN), Australian Business Number (ABN) and GST registration.[13]

If a partnership is dissolved or a partner leaves, it is an unusual law in Victoria that a notice be put in the Government Gazette and at least one newspaper in each district where the partnership carries on business.[14]

How is a partnership taxed?

The partnership is not taxed, instead each partner is individually taxed on their share of the partnership profit.

The profit of the partnership is determined by the revenue of the partnership less business expenses.

The default position is that the partners are entitled to equally share in the profit[15], however, this can be changed if the partners all agree[16].

What are the pros and cons of being in a partnership?

Like a sole trader, a partnership is easy to set up. Technically, all you need to do is register an ABN. That said, to make sure all the partners are on the same page, you should enter into a partnership agreement, which should really be done through a lawyer.

A big negative for partnerships is the lack of personal asset protection. This is even worse than for a sole trader, because not only are you personally liable for the debts you incur in the partnership, you are also liable for debts incurred by the other partners in the course of the partnership business.

There is some flexibility to distribute income, but only amongst the partners, which is usually not that helpful in minimising tax.

Generally, the maximum numbers of partners you can have is 20[17], but this increases if you are in one of the select professions which allow for higher numbers, such as doctors, lawyers and accountants.

When to use a partnership?

If you are going into business with other people, a partnership is by far the easiest option to set up.

Your big problem is your personal exposure, both to the actions of the other partners in the course of the business, and to the business as a whole.

Partnership rating

Feature	Rating (1 = bad, 5 = good)
Cost	★★★★
Ease	★★★★
Asset protection	★
Tax minimisation	★★
Flexibility	★★★

Companies

Explain it to me like I'm a 10-year-old...

A company is most like the genie in Aladdin. When the young boy rubs the bottle, the genie pops out; and when the owners register with ASIC, the company pops out.

I am talking about the 1992 animation Aladdin movie with Robin Williams' voice as the crazy blue ghost Aladdin, not the 2019 Will Smith Aladdin. This is important because a company is a bit like a ghost in that it does exist, it has a name and can do things like enter into contracts or employ people – basically anything its masters (the directors) tell it to do, but at the same time it does not have a physical body.

The point is that once a company is registered, it becomes its own real entity, like the genie. Of course, the master owns and controls the company, but the company still exists on its own. This is great because it means that you can get the company to do whatever you want, and, as long as you do not get it to do anything illegal, if the company happens to get in trouble, it is the company who has to face the music, not you – just like the genie.

The other thing about genies and companies is that they never really die. Sure, the genie can be put back in the bottle or the company can be deregistered, but a quick rub on the bottle or an application to ASIC and, *magic*, they are back again.

Now for my first wish…

What is a company?

A company is a completely made-up concept and only exists because the law says it can.

A company comes into existence when it is registered with the Australian Securities and Investment Commission (ASIC)[18], at which point it becomes a legal entity. What this means is that, in the eyes of the law, a company is a living breathing individual that can do everything a business needs to do; buy things, sell things, enter into contracts, sue and be sued. What is significant is that the company is separate from the owners (the shareholders) and the people who control the company (the directors) – it is a separate legal entity.

The concept of separate legal entity

The fundamental principle behind companies is that they are a separate legal entity.[19] This means that from a legal perspective, a company is effectively its own person. It can do everything a sole trader or a partnership can do – enter into contracts, employ staff, buy stuff, sell stuff, whatever is needed to run the business.

What is unique is that, unlike a partnership where all the individual partners are personally part of the partnership, in a company, the people that run the company (the directors) and the people that own the company (the shareholders) are not personally part of the company in its day to day operations. Sure, the directors and the shareholders have their role in determining what the company does, but it is just a role.

An example might help explain the significance of this. Say I register a company. I make myself the only director and the only shareholder. As the director of my new company, I then go to you to buy $1m worth of stock which you sell to my company on credit. My company sells the stock to someone else but because of some other bad business deals, the company ends up having no money to pay you back for your stock. You then turn to me saying that because I am the director and shareholder, I should be personally responsible for the money. I am not.

Because the company is a separate legal entity, I have no personal responsibility for the money.

An extension of this concept is that just because you own the shares in the company, does not mean that you own the assets of the company.[20] Even if you are the sole director and only shareholder of a company, that does not give you a right to, say, help yourself to the company vehicle or the company bank account. In fact, if you were to do so, you would be in breach of your director duties to act in good faith and proper purpose in the interests of the company.[21]

If you can get your head around this idea of a company being its own entity, completely separate from the shareholders and directors, it will help you understand how all the rest works.

Ultimately, it is because of this concept of companies being a separate legal entity that they are so popular and prominent in business today. Think about it, you can own a business or a part of a business (as a shareholder) and if the business gets into trouble, all you have to worry about is your original investment.

If you are a director there are other possible risks, such as claims for insolvent trading – more about that later.

Shareholders' limited liability

You have probably seen the word '*Limited*' or '*Ltd*' at the end of a company name. That means that the liability of the shareholders is limited to any unpaid amount owing on the shares.[22] All this means is that if you have not fully paid for the shares, you remain liable for that shortfall.

Here is an example. Say the company issued 10 new shares for $1 each.

If you bought those shares and paid the company the full $10, you would have no ongoing liability. So, if the company went bust, you would not owe any money at all.

If, however, you only paid $4, you would still owe the company $6, and if the company went bust, you would be liable to the company for that $6.

How does a company work?

The directors are responsible for running the business.[23]

To get things done, the directors can enter into contracts on behalf of the company.[24] If there is more than one director, the contracts need to be signed by at least two directors or a director and a company secretary.

If they want, the directors can appoint one of the directors to be the managing director to run the business for them.[25] If appointed, a managing director can sign contracts on behalf of the company on his or her own.

The directors can also appoint an agent to enter into contracts on behalf of the company.[26] If you are going to enter into a contract with an 'agent' of the company, you need to make sure that person has been properly appointed by the directors. You should get written authority from the directors to confirm this.

The shareholders are responsible for choosing the directors.[27] They can also choose when to remove a director[28] and can choose what they pay the directors.[29]

To make formal decisions, the directors and the shareholders have their own meetings in which they pass resolutions.[30]

Constitutions and shareholders agreements

The Corporations Act includes a whole stack of rules on how a company is to be run. These are called the Replaceable Rules. They include things like what percentage of votes are needed to appoint a director and how to run directors' meetings and shareholders' meetings.

They are call the Replaceable Rules because they can be replaced. The Replaceable Rules are the default rules. They apply to the company until a company decides to have its own rules, which it does by adopting a constitution.[31]

A constitution might include a change like, where the Replaceable Rules provide that you need over 50% of the shareholders vote to appoint a director, the constitution might change that rule to be that if you have over 25% of the shares you are entitled to appoint a director.

The Replaceable Rules and the constitution work as a contract between the company and each director and each shareholder, and between the shareholders themselves.[32] This allows those involved to be able to enforce the rules.

Some companies go a step further and adopt a

shareholders' agreement. This is just a further contract between the shareholders that sits above the constitution and Replaceable Rules. Shareholders' agreements can be useful in dealing with things like, what is to happen if a shareholder retires or dies.

Usually, if a shareholder dies, their shares would go to whoever they are left to in their Will. For small companies, it may not be suitable for the deceased's family to suddenly have a controlling interest in the company. A shareholders' agreement might provide that if a shareholder dies, their shares automatically get sold to the remaining shareholders.

While both constitutions and shareholders' agreements can be useful, if you are going to adopt either, you need to make sure that you do not unnecessarily change what is a good working arrangement in the first place.

Making directors responsible

As I said earlier, in a partnership, if a partner does something wrong, all the partners are jointly responsible. In a company, however, because it is separate from the directors and shareholders, if the company does something wrong, the directors and shareholders are not personally responsible.

The problem is that as a society we need to make sure that companies are responsible. We need to make sure they do not rip people off, that they look after their employees and generally conduct business properly. Because a company does not have a physical body, the only way you can punish a company is by issuing a fine. If the company has no money to start with, there is not much you can do.

Therefore, the only way to really make a company responsible is to make the people that control the company (the directors) personally responsible. And that is what the law is increasingly trying to do.

As well as laws requiring directors to act in the best interests of the company[33], there are ever increasing laws that make directors personally responsible for things like employee entitlements[34], occupational health and safety[35], PAYG, GST and superannuation obligations[36], environment protection[37] and anti-competitive behaviour[38].

What these laws do not do is make directors responsible for debts owed by the company, unless they were incurred when the company did not have enough money to pay its debts, which is called insolvent trading. [39] Insolvent trading is discussed in more detail below.

Before you get excited with the idea of making your grandmother the sole director so you can avoid personal liability, you should be aware that you can still be considered a director if you act in the position of director, what they call a 'de facto director', or if you control the real directors, what they call a 'shadow director'.[40]

Director's Guarantees

Of course, many businesspeople understand that directors are not personally responsible for the debts of the company, so when dealing with another company, they will often insist on the director or directors providing a personal guarantee for the company.

Suddenly the director will be personally responsible for money that is owed or becomes owed by the company to that other business.

Talk about ruining the limited liability party!

Insolvent trading

The Achilles heel of a director's responsibility (or lack of responsibility) for a company that goes bust is the insolvent trading laws. Simply, a director has a duty to prevent a company from incurring a debt if the debt is likely to make the company insolvent.[41] This can even be a criminal offence if done dishonestly.[42]

The tricky part of this law is working out when a company is insolvent. The law says that a company is insolvent if it is unable to pay its debts when they become due.[43] Of course, businesses will go through lean periods, but that does not necessarily mean that the company is insolvent. To help determine this you need to look at the company's assets and liabilities as a whole. If you are unable to pay your bills, you need to consider whether additional money could be raised or whether you have any surplus assets that could be quickly sold off.[44]

One important point to keep in mind is that if a company fails to keep proper financial records and there is a question of insolvency, if you cannot prove otherwise, it will be assumed that the company was insolvent.[45]

Directors being bullies

One of the challenges with how companies work is that power and control are largely determined by who owns the most shares. If you have most of the shares, you can appoint the directors, who ultimately control what the company does, including how much to pay the directors. Do you see the problem? This leaves a lot of scope for majority shareholders to push their weight around and do things that might not be good for the other shareholders.

This is a common problem and there are laws that help those minority shareholders. The main one is the law that allows minority shareholders to get the Court to intervene if the company is being run in a way that is contrary to the interests of the shareholders as a whole, or if the company is being oppressive, unfairly prejudicial or unfairly discriminatory against a shareholder[46] - basically if the directors are being bullies.

If the Court decides that a director is being oppressive, the Court has a wide discretion around what it can do, including forcing one party to buy out another or even wind-up the company.[47]

How to set up a company?

Unlike a partnership which comes into existence when the partners start working in the partnership, a company comes into existence when it is registered with ASIC (Australian Securities & Investments Commission).

To register a proprietary or private company in Australia you need at least one shareholder (also called a member)[48] and one director who must be over 18 and a resident of Australia.[49]

It is a pretty easy process to create a company – you can just go online, fill in the details and pay your fee and Bob's your uncle. You will be issued with an ACN (Australian Company Number) and your company is alive!

You will need to get the initial directors to sign a consent to being a director[50]. Plus, before you can start trading, you will need to get an ABN.

You may want to get a Registered Business Name if you are going to trade with a name different to the company name.

Like the ABN, the company name or registered business name (whichever you adopt) and the ACN need to be displayed at every business premises open to the public[51] and on all public documents[52].

If your ACN is the same as the last nine digits of your ABN, you are allowed to just use the ABN, instead of both.[53]

Ending a company

An unusual feature of companies is that they can continue forever. If a director dies, another one can be appointed, and if a shareholder dies, their shares will usually go to their estate.[54]

A company can be deregistered if it is no longer being used[55], or if ASIC decides because it has not complied with its obligations.[56]

However, there is also scope for a company to be reinstated.[57] This means that technically, a company never really dies.

How is a company taxed?

Because a company is its own entity, it is taxed like a normal person, except that instead of being taxed at a different rate depending on the amount of income (marginal rate), a company is taxed at a fixed percentage of 27.5% for small companies (having an annual turnover of less than $25m[58]) and 30% for bigger companies. Please note that these tax rates may change from time to time.

To get the profit out to the owners of the company (the shareholders), the company will declare a dividend. That dividend then becomes personal income for the shareholders, which they will have to include in their own tax returns.

Because the company has already paid tax on the profit, in Australia for Australian companies, shareholders are allowed to get a tax credit, so they only end up paying tax on the profit based on their own marginal tax rate, rather than the company tax rate.

The pros and cons of being a company

As you have hopefully picked up, one of the main reasons for using a company is that you can have lots of owners who should not have any liability or ongoing responsibility if the company mucks up. Sure, they might lose their investment, but otherwise, they simply walk away.

The directors also largely avoid any ongoing personal responsibility. While they need to be careful, as long as they manage the business properly and do not do anything silly, they too will have no personal liability if the business fails.

Other great things about a company is its flexibility to allow shareholders to come and go by simply transferring shares and its ability to keep going forever.

When to use a company?

Companies are useful for providing personal protection in case the business goes pear-shaped. They are also good to allow other people to invest in the business but not necessarily run the business.

They do not, however, provide flexibility to choose to whom to distribute the income.

Company rating

Feature	Rating (1 = bad, 5 = good)
Cost	★★
Ease	★★★
Asset protection	★★★★
Tax minimisation	★★
Flexibility	★★★★★

Ernie Pty Ltd

As you might recall, Ernie Duncan wants to enter into a big supply contract with you.

Remember that when you enter into a contract with another business, it is the **entity** who will sign the contract and who will ultimately be responsible for their side of the deal.

In the case of Ernie Duncan, the **entity** will be the company, Ernie Pty Ltd, that will enter into the contract. Because Ernie is the sole director of the company, the contract should be signed by him in that capacity.

You should now understand that, unless the company was trading insolvent, even though Ernie is the sole director and sole shareholder of the company, he will not be personally responsible for any debts of the company, including any money the company owes you.

Different structure types

Now it is time to think about what it means for Ernie Pty Ltd to be acting as trustee of The Ernie Unit Trust.

We also need to work out what it means for Ernie to own all the units in The Ernie Unit Trust as trustee for The Ernie Family Trust.

This is the step of understanding the **structure** of a business.

To do this we will first look at how trusts work. This includes both unit trusts and discretionary trusts.

Once you get your head around trusts, we will look at combination structures. This is where different entity types and trusts are used to make complicated structures, like Ernie's, where you have a company, then a unit trust, then an individual, then a discretionary trust.

Trusts

Explain it to me like I'm a 10-year-old...

A trust is like The Smurfs, with all the different little Smurfs, like Clumsy Smurf, Brainy Smurf, Hefty Smurf and Smurfette, who all live in the secret Smurf Village in their cute mushroom-shaped houses in the forest.

Of course, looking after the Smurfs is Papa Smurf.

Papa Smurf is like the trustee of the Smurf Trust. He owns all the Smurf Village, but he owns it for the benefit of the Smurfs, who would be the beneficiaries of the Smurf Trust.

If Gargamel wanted to buy the Smurf Village then he would have to buy it from Papa Smurf. Even though Papa Smurf owns the Smurf Village, any money that Papa Smurf received from Gargamel would have to go to the Smurfs.

If the Smurf Trust was a discretionary trust, Papa Smurf could choose which Smurf or Smurfs to give the money to, mostly likely to the ones who need it, like Lazy Smurf and Clumsy Smurf.

If the Smurf Trust was a unit trust and all the Smurfs were unit holders, then Papa Smurf would have to share the money with all the Smurfs.

There are some obvious problems with this explanation.

Firstly, there is no way that Papa Smurf would ever sell the Smurf Village to that scumbag, Gargamel.

Secondly, even if he did sell the Smurf Village, it would not be for money, because we all know that Smurfs do not use money, because they consider friendship and family to be more valuable than personal possessions.

Now that I think about it, trusts are not much like the Smurfs after all.

What is a trust?

Trusts were originally used when property was left to a child. The property would be transferred to an adult (**trustee**) on the basis they hold the property for the benefit of the child (**beneficiary**).

This concept has evolved to be used by families and businesses to protect assets and to pay less tax.

What can be confusing about trusts is that people naturally think that a trust is an entity on its own, like sole traders, partnerships and companies. This is not correct.

A trust is just an arrangement where the trustee is required to act in the interests of the beneficiaries.

One way to help get your head around this is to think about the process of entering into a contract. As discussed above, a sole trader or individual can sign a contract themselves, any one of the partners can sign a contract on behalf of the partnership, and the directors can sign a contract on behalf of the company. A trust, on the other hand, cannot sign a contract because it is not an entity. Instead, it is the trustee (being an individual, partnership or company) who signs the contract. And it is the trustee who is ultimately responsible for the contract. It is just that they have to act for the benefit of the beneficiaries of the trust.

Types of trusts

There are two main types of trusts used in business — unit trust and discretionary trust.

Unit trusts

A unit trust is a little bit like a company, in that the beneficiaries of a unit trust own individual units, like how a shareholder will own shares.

Owning a unit in a unit trust entitles the unit holder to the income and assets of the trust in proportion to the number of units they hold. For example, if there are 5 units in the trust and you hold 1 unit, then you are entitled to 20% of the trust property.

When distributing the assets and income of the trust, the trustee does not have any choice as to which of the unit holders to distribute any money or assets, it must be done to the unit holders in proportion to their share of units.

Discretionary trusts

A discretionary trust is a trust where the trustee has the discretion or choice to choose from a range of beneficiaries. This obviously different to a unit trust where the beneficiaries are fixed.

Discretionary trusts are commonly used for family groups, in which case the definition of beneficiary could include the husband and wife, their children and their extended family.

What this means is that when distributing the assets or income of the trust, the trustee can choose whomever they want to distribute to, so long as they fall within the definition of beneficiary.

This can be great for families because it means that the trustee can distribute income to members of the family who are otherwise earning less income and on a lower tax bracket, so they pay less tax.

How does a trust work?

To make sure the trust arrangement operates smoothly, the trust usually comes with a whole lot of rules which are contained in the **trust deed**.

If a person or company is a trustee of a trust, rather than doing what is best for themselves or, in the case of a company, their shareholders, everything they do in their role as trustee must be what is best for the beneficiaries. If the trustee makes any income, it must go to the beneficiaries. If the trustee wants to distribute an asset, it must be given to the beneficiaries or sold with the proceeds going to the beneficiaries.

In the case of a business, it is the trustee that is the person or company that owns and controls the business. It is the trustee who enters into contracts, who buys and sells the stock, and who employs the staff. It is also the trustee who is responsible for any debts or liabilities of the business.

Dealing with another trust

There are two common oversights when doing business with another trust.

The first oversight is when a party tries to enter into a contract as '*The Trustee* for The ABC Trust ABN 12 345 678 910', without specifying the actual trustee. In this case it is not clear which entity is entering into the contract and, as a result, which entity will be responsible for completing the contract.

The second oversight is entering into a contract with a company or individual not appreciating that they are acting in the capacity of trustee of a trust.

Both oversights can be problematic if things go wrong and the contract needs to be enforced, as both could alter who and what you could potentially have recourse against.

Steps to overcome these oversights are provided in Part 2 – Identification.

A trustee's right of indemnity

So a trustee is not left out of pocket, the trustee usually has a right of indemnity from the assets of the trust.[59] This means that if the trustee incurs debts or owes money while running the business, the trustee can use the trust money or assets to pay for them.

In the case of a unit trust, the trustee's right of indemnity can also extend to the unitholders.[60] This means that a unitholder could potentially be personally liable for the debts of the trust.

There is scope, however, for a trust deed to limit or even cancel the trustee's right of indemnity.[61] This can apply to both the right of indemnity from the assets of the trust and from the unitholders.

Hopefully, you appreciate the significance of this point.

If you are dealing with a trust, you need to appreciate that while a trustee can incur debts on behalf of the trust, the trustee may not necessarily be able to use the trust assets and money to pay the debt. If the trustee is a company with no assets of its own, you are going to be in trouble.

On the flip side, if you are a beneficiary of a unit trust, you also need to be careful that the trustee does not have a right of indemnity against the unitholders, in which case you could be personally liable for the debts and liabilities of the trust.

To make matters more challenging, the only way to find out if a trustee's right of indemnity has been limited is by checking the trust deed.

How to set up a trust?

To set up a trust you need is someone independent of the trust (not a potential beneficiary) to put in some money (could just be $10) and declare that money to be held on trust. That person is called the **settlor**. This initial contribution is necessary to create the trust because there must be an initial subject matter of the trust.

The trust arrangement is usually confirmed in the trust deed which includes the rules of the trust, who are the beneficiaries or potential beneficiaries (in the case of a discretionary trust) and who is to control the trust (the trustee).

The trust deed might also include an **appointor**, this person or people get to choose who is the trustee. Because of this power, it is the appointor who would have ultimate control over the trust.

In Victoria, setting up a trust (a declaration of trust) is a dutiable transaction. This means that you have to pay duty (formerly called stamp duty) to the State Revenue Office. As long as the declaration of trust does not declare a trust over land, the current duty is a $200.[62]

Unlike a company where you have the certainty of being able to register through ASIC, a trust relies on the people involved to keep records and be able to prove its existence. Because of this, it is extremely important that if you do set up a trust, you go to great lengths to ensure you keep and maintain all documents and records.

It also means that it can be difficult to find out about someone else's trust. At the end of the day, all you can really do is to try and get a copy of the trust deed.

Ending a trust

The trust deed will usually include rules around how and when a trust can be brought to an end.

A trust can also be wound-up with the consent of all beneficiaries or by distributing all the trust property to the beneficiaries.[63]

One important note is that the law prevents a trust from lasting forever. In Victoria, the longest a trust can go for is 80 years.[64] At the end of the 80 years the trust must be wound-up.

Eighty-years may seem like a long time, but it is not really in the scheme of a successful multi-generational family business.

How is a trust taxed?

Because a trust is not an entity, it cannot be personally taxed. So how does the Australian Taxation Office (ATO) get its pound of flesh?

Income generated through a trust is usually distributed by the trustee to the beneficiaries to be included in their personal income.[65]

If the income is not distributed to the beneficiaries, then the income is usually taxed as income of the trustee, but at a flat rate of 45%[66].

Unit trusts

For a unit trust, the income is usually distributed to the beneficiaries in proportion of their units. If a beneficiary owns half the units, they are entitled to half the income. Alternatively, the income can be accumulated by the trustee and taxed to the beneficiary.

A significant feature of unit trusts is that they receive capital gains tax discounts[67] that companies do not. This is one of the reasons why unit trusts are sometimes used instead of straight companies when there is property involved.

On the flip side, however, land held in a trust can incur higher land tax.[68]

Discretionary trusts

For a discretionary trust, it is up to the trustee to choose to which beneficiary or beneficiaries to distribute the income and how much.

Being able to choose where to distribute the income is one of the key features of a discretionary trust. Usually for a discretionary trust the potential beneficiaries are wide. Often the trust deed will define the beneficiaries to include the primary beneficiaries, this might be the husband and wife for whom the trust was set up, then it could include all their family – their parents, siblings, children and grandchildren, plus related entities. When it comes to tax time, the trustee can distribute the income to anyone who falls within that group.

What this means is that if there is someone in the group that has not earned much income for that financial year, the trustee can distribute the income to them and they would not pay much tax. Whereas, if there was someone who has already earned lots of income, the trustee could avoid distributing the trust income to them.

Where this works well is if you have a married couple where one is working and the other is not. The working person would be taxed on the income they earn from their job, whereas the person who is not working would start with no income. In that situation, the income generated through the trust can be distributed to the person who is not working which would result in a much better tax outcome than if the trust income had been paid on top of the working person's income.

Back in the good old days, married couples would get their young children involved by distributing the income to them. Usually the young children would not have earnt any other income so the family would end up paying heaps less tax. The ATO has long cottoned onto this arrangement and now any income earned by minors above $416 is taxed at 45%.[69]

One exception to this rule is income distributed through a testamentary trust (which is a trust in a Will). In that situation, children are treated as adults for the purpose of trust distributions.[70]

Author's note about trusts and tax

I have done my best to try and explain things on a high level, however, the tax laws dealing with trusts are extremely complicated and this book is not intended to cover all tax issues associated with trusts.

If you are going to run your business through a trust, be sure to get professional tax advice.

The pros and cons of using a trust

The main reasons to use a trust are for asset protection and for tax minimisation.

From an asset protection perspective, trusts can be effectively used to protect both the assets of the trust and of the beneficiaries of the trust.

In the right situation, using a discretionary trust to be able to choose to whom income is paid can have considerable tax benefits.

The negatives of trusts are the complexity and cost.

As you may have picked-up, trusts can be complicated, with trust deeds to work through and new rules to understand.

There are costs involved with setting up and operating a trust, plus they really need to be done through your lawyer and accountant which will incur fees.

When to use a trust?

A discretionary trust provides the best flexibility for choosing who to distribute income. But if you are going into business with someone else, a discretionary trust on its own does not provide the beneficiaries with any fixed interest or ownership in the business. This could be an absolute minefield if something happens to one of the business owners or there is a falling out.

A unit trust does not provide flexibility to choose to whom to distribute the income, but there can be tax advantages when compared to companies, particularly if there is property owned in the trust.

If you are going to use a trust, you should avoid having individuals as trustees because they will be personally liable for the debts of the trust.

Trust rating

Feature	Rating (1 = bad, 5 = good)
Cost	★ ★
Ease	★
Asset protection	★ ★ ★ ★
Tax minimisation	★ ★ ★ ★
Flexibility	★ ★ ★

Ernie Pty Ltd as trustee for The Ernie Unit Trust

If you recall, Ernie Pty Ltd is acting as trustee for The Ernie Unit Trust.

This means that everything Ernie Pty Ltd does in its capacity as trustee of the trust must be for the benefit of the unit trust.

Any assets the company owns, it holds them for the benefit of the unit holders of the trust.

Any income the company makes, it must be distributed to the unit holders.

Because The Ernie Unit Trust is a unit trust, it means that the interest of the beneficiaries is fixed. In this case, Ernie is the sole unit holder, so 100% of the assets or income of the trust must be distributed to Ernie. If there were two unit holders, they would each be entitled to 50% of the proceeds of the trust.

So it turns out that Ernie Pty Ltd as trustee for The Ernie Unit Trust owes you a shed-load of money and will not pay it back. At the same time, it owns a property that could cover the debt. The question is whether you can sue Ernie Pty Ltd and force the sale of the property to pay for your debt.

As explained earlier, unless The Ernie Unit Trust Deed denies Ernie Pty Ltd a right to the assets of the trust (**right of indemnity**), then you could potentially get your hands on the property.

If the Trust Deed specifically denies Ernie Pty Ltd a right to the assets of the trust to pay for its debts, then you are unlikely to get your hands on that property and as a result you are unlikely to get your money back.

Combination structures

So, there you have it – sole traders, partnerships and companies are your core entities and trusts provide an option for an arrangement below those entities.

The problem is that all of the entities and trusts have their pros and cons.

To utilise the benefits of the different options and to avoid the problems, you can adopt a mix and match approach. Here goes…

Option 1
Discretionary trust with company trustee

A common structure to use is combining a discretionary trust with a company. This is the classic combination structure often used for families, and would look like this:

> ➢ Your Family Pty Ltd as trustee for Your Family Trust

This would include the following:

Company	Your Family Pty Ltd
Directors	You
Shareholders	You
Trust	Your Family Trust
Beneficiaries	You and your family

Why use this structure?

The problem with discretionary trusts is that the trustee is personally liable for the debts of the trust. This means that if you are personally the trustee, while you have the flexibility to distribute the income and assets to your family, you are personally responsible for the debts of the trust.

Instead of having an individual as the trustee, you can set up a company to take on that role. You can still be the director and shareholder of the company, which means you still get to control things, but because the company is a separate legal entity, you should not be personally liable for the debts if things go wrong.

While this structure is great for a single family, if a business involves other people then it is not so great. As discussed earlier, the problem is that the beneficiaries do not have a fixed interest in the trust, and it is ultimately up to the trustee to decide to which of the beneficiaries it is paid. This could be a big problem if there are multiple owners from different families.

Option 2 Company owned by family trusts

If you are going into business with another person, a common structure to use is a company, but instead of owning the shares in the company yourself, you own the shares in the structure above, being a discretionary trust with a company trustee. This would look like this:

➢ Our Business Pty Ltd

This would include the following:

Company	Our Business Pty Ltd
Directors	You Your business partner
Shareholders	Your Family Pty Ltd as trustee for Your Family Trust (*see Option 1*) Your business partner or his/her chosen entity

Why use this structure?

The benefits of using a company to own and run the business is that it provides asset protection for the shareholders, plus it is easy to add more owners into the mix by simply selling or issuing shares in the company.

Using your own discretionary trust with company trustee to own the shares means that you have the flexibility to choose to whom in your family to distribute the revenue generated by the company once it flows out as dividends. This means that you could distribute it to any low-income earners and pay less tax.

The challenges of this structure are the cost and the ease. You will need to set up and operate the main company and you also need your own trustee company and your own discretionary trust.

Option 3 Unit trust held by family trusts

This structure adds another layer to Option 2 and is sometimes used for property developments involving multiple parties.

The controlling entity is a company, but it operates solely for the benefit of the unitholders. It is the unitholders who effectively own the business.

The trustee company still has shareholders, but the shares are not worth anything because everything goes to the unitholders.

To take advantages of benefits of Option 1, the units are held in the parties' own family trusts.

From the outside, this structure would look like this:

- Our Business Pty Ltd as trustee for Our Business Unit Trust

This would include the following:

Company	Our Business Pty Ltd
Directors	You Your business partner
Shareholders	Your Family Pty Ltd as trustee for Your Family Trust (*see Option 1*) Your business partner or his/her chosen entity
Trust	Our Business Unit Trust
Unitholders	Your Family Pty Ltd as trustee for Your Family Trust (*see Option 1*) Your business partner or his/her chosen entity

Why use this structure?

This structure is sometimes used if the business has multiple owners and involves buying and selling property. This is because of the capital gains tax advantages trusts get that companies do not.

The negative side of this option, when compared to Option 2, is the added level of complexity and cost involved with having a unit trust.

Option 4 Partnership of family trusts

A final option is to set up a partnership, but instead of personally being a partner, you use your discretionary trust to be the partner in your place. In this case, your business partner would probably want to set up their own discretionary trust. The partnership would be called:

> Your Family Pty Ltd as trustee for Your Family Trust and Your Business Partner Pty Ltd as trustee for Your Business Partner Family Trust Partnership

This would include the following:

Partners	Your Family Pty Ltd as trustee for Your Family Trust (*see Option 1*)
	Your Business Partner Pty Ltd as trustee for Your Business Partner Family Trust

Why to use this structure?

The benefit of this structure is that you get the personal protection from your trust arrangement, plus you and the other partner or partners have the flexibility to decide on how to split the income of the business between you.

This structure can also be easier to access capital gains tax concessions when compared to companies and unit trusts.

A downside is that it is harder to add and remove owners, when compared to the other structures. Plus, other businesses may have reservations about dealing with this unusual structure.

Ernie Pty Ltd as trustee for The Ernie Unit Trust with units held by Ernie as trustee for The Ernie Family Trust

You might recall that the above structure owes you a shed-load of money.

In the previous example, I mentioned that Ernie Pty Ltd as trustee for The Ernie Unit Trust owns a property which could cover your debt. Turns out I was wrong, and that actually, the property is owned by Ernie in his capacity as trustee for The Ernie Family Trust.

You still want to sue Ernie and the question is still whether you can get your hands on that property.

Are you ready for a bit of a head spin? Here goes...

Firstly, let have a look at this situation on the basis that neither The Ernie Unit Trust Deed nor The Ernie Family Trust Deed limits the trustee's right of indemnity (their right to assets of the trust or the unitholders).

You sue Ernie Pty Ltd who potentially has a right of indemnity from the unitholders of The Ernie Unit Trust, being Ernie.

Now Ernie owes you the money, but that does not mean you get your hands on the property because the property is owned by Ernie as trustee for The Ernie Family Trust.

Because The Ernie Family Trust is a discretionary trust, none of the beneficiaries has a fixed interest in the trust which means that even though Ernie could potentially be a beneficiary of the trust, this is not fixed and as a result neither Ernie nor any of the other beneficiaries owe any rights of indemnity.

This means that at the end of the day, you cannot get your hands the property!

If either of the Trust Deeds limit any rights of indemnity, then that will put a further block into any claim against the property. But that does not matter, because you are not getting it anyway!

Final comment about structures

As you may have picked up, the above structures are complicated. They deal with layers of documentation, a number of different laws, some laws federal and some state, and differing tax consequences to navigate. Quite simply, each of the above options has the capacity to be a legal and tax minefield.

Hopefully, this book will help you understand how the different structures work and why you might use them. It is certainly not attempting to substitute good legal and accounting assistance, which I consider to be essential.

Other common business arrangements

Joint ventures

Joint ventures do not really fall under business structures, but I think it is important to mention them.

A joint venture is a contractual arrangement where two or more separate entities will work together on a specific project for their own individual gains.[71] Being a contractual arrangement, the terms and conditions of the joint venture are contained in the joint venture agreement.

A joint venture can sometimes look a bit like a partnership, in that it is a group of people or companies that work together to make money. What is different is that the joint venture is usually limited to a specific project and the parties do not have an intention to come together to form a combined entity. Usually, the parties to a joint venture want to stay completely separate for the purposes of responsibility and liability.

When you consider how easy it is to set up a partnership, the real challenge with setting up a joint venture is making sure you do not inadvertently fall into being a partnership. This is where the joint venture agreement plays an important role in dictating what the relationship is between the parties and how it will all play out.

If you are wanting to set up a joint venture, you should get legal advice.

If you are dealing with a joint venture, you need to be clear as to which entity or entities you are dealing with.

Franchises

Franchises are also not a business structure but should also probably be mentioned.

Most people would be familiar with franchises, such as McDonalds. What some people do not appreciate is that when you go into a McDonalds, you are not buying a burger from the global McDonalds corporation, you are buying a burger from the franchisee. The franchisee is most likely a small company set up by the person that runs that particular store.

As a franchisee, that small company has a franchise agreement with the global McDonalds corporation to use the McDonalds brand and to sell and market the McDonalds products the way McDonalds tells them.[72] That is all.

To help the franchisees, the law has developed the Franchising Code of Conduct[73]. This provides rules for setting up and running franchises, particularly around what information a franchisor has to disclose to a franchisee, such as costs involved, and what franchisees can do if they have a dispute.

Franchises probably warrant a whole book on their own. For the purpose of this book, the key take away is that if you are dealing with a franchise, you need to focus on the entity you are dealing with, the franchisee, and not get distracted by the franchisor, no matter how impressive they may be.

PART 2
IDENTIFICATION

Business identifiers

Now that you hopefully understand the different types of entities and structures, your next challenge is to identify these when you are dealing with another business. The three main identifiers of a business are through its Australian Business Number (ABN), Registered Business Name and, if you are dealing with a company, its Australian Company Number (ACN). They each serve a different purpose and are often all needed to properly identify a business.

The other thing you need to consider is how to identify individual people. Unfortunately, these days you cannot simply take someone for who they say they are.

Australian Business Numbers (ABNs)

An ABN is a unique 11-digit number that identifies a business to the government and the community.

One of the main purposes of ABNs is to identify businesses for taxation purposes.[74]

An ABN must be included on all tax invoices, receipts and orders. It is an offence if a business fails to do so.[75]

If you are dealing with a business that does not provide an ABN, it is generally your responsibility to withhold tax at a rate of 46.5%.[76] Regardless of whether you withhold that tax or not, your business could end up owning that money to the Australian Taxation Office (ATO). There are some exceptions to this rule, including if the payment is less than $50.[1]

---

[1] There are some exceptions to this rule, including if the payment is less than $50 or such higher amount prescribed by the GST Act or the supply is wholly input taxed. *Taxation Administration Act 1953* (Cth), Schedule 1, s 12-190(4).

The penalty is two-years imprisonment if someone misuses an ABN[77], such as using a number that is not an ABN as if it were an ABN or using another business's ABN.

ABNs are registered through the Australian Government - Australian Business Register (https://abr.gov.au/).

Searching a business's ABN should be your first step in identifying a business. This can be done through the Australian Government's ABN Lookup page (https://abr.business.gov.au/). This is a free search.

The search will tell you whether the ABN is active and give you your first clue as to what sort of entity and structure you are dealing with.

Because ABNs are mainly for tax purposes, they sometimes only provide limited information about an entity or structure, particularly when dealing with trusts.

When dealing with a trust, it is not uncommon for the entity name to state, '*The Trustee for the ABC Family Trust*' and the entity type to state '*Discretionary Trading Trust*'. As we now know, a trust is not an entity so really this is incorrect. This limited information is fine for tax purposes because it is the trust structure that determines the tax, not the trustee entity. However, if you want to sue that business, just knowing the name and structure of the trust is of limited help. If you are going to sue a trust structure, you need to sue the trustee entity. For this reason, you also need to consider the next two identifiers.

Business names

It is the law in Australia that all businesses must include its name on all written business communications[78] and it must be displayed prominently at every place of business open to the public[79].

For the purpose of identifying a business, a business can use its own actual name. In the case of a sole trader, this would be her or his own name, or if a partnership, then all the partners' names, or if a company, the company's registered name, which would usually include 'Pty Ltd' on the end.[80]

However, if a business wants to trade under a different name, it can only do so if it registers that name. In fact, it is an offence to carry on a business with a different name that is not registered.[81]

Business name registration is done through ASIC (Australian Securities and Investment Commission) (www.asic.gov.au).

Because the Business Name Register is now Australia-wide, when registering a name, one of the common challenges is making sure a name, or something similar, is not already taken.

One important thing to keep in mind is that registering a business name does not give the registered owner any special protection or rights to that name.[82] While it may stop others from registering the same or similar name, it would not stop others using it for other reasons, such as for a product or brand. If a business wants to protect a name, it should register a trademark.

If a business is using a name that is not its own actual name, then a business name search should be your second step in identifying that business. This is done through the Business Name Register at ASIC Connect (https://asic.gov.au/online-services/search-asics-registers/business-names/). This is also a free search.

This search will identify the entity that has registered the name which will help you confirm that you have the right ABN and ACN for the business you think you are dealing with.

Australian Company Numbers (ACN)

As you would expect, ACNs only apply to companies. When a company is registered it is given its ACN, a 9-digit number used to identify the company. Because company names can be changed quite easily, the ACN is a more important identifier than the company name.

Like the ABN, the ACN needs to be displayed at every business premises open to the public[83] and on all public documents[84], however, if a company's ACN is the same as the last nine digits of its ABN, it is allowed to display just the ABN, instead of both the ABN and the ACN.[85]

An ACN search should tell you all the important information about a company, including its registered address, its directors and secretary and its shareholders (or members). This search can be done through ASIC Connect (https://connectonline.asic.gov.au/). This is a paid search.

While this search is terrific for identifying a company, it will not tell you if the company is acting in the capacity of a trustee of a trust. The best way to find that out is through the ABN search.

Verification of identity

If you buy or sell a property these days, you may be surprised at the extent of identification required under the Verification of Identity Standard.[86] I mention the Standard because it is the benchmark for verifying someone's identity.

Some of the key features of the Standard are:

- the verification must be done face-to-face,[87]
- the documents used to verify a person must be originals,[88]
- the documents must be current, except for an expired Australian Passport which must have expired within the last two years,
- the preferred documents are[89]:
    - Australian passport, *plus*
    - Australian drivers licence, *plus*
    - change of name or marriage certificate if necessary.
- As a last resort, the person can get someone who is not a relative and has known the person for over 12 months to help verify their identify.

If you are not able to verify someone's identity yourself, you can arrange for the other person to have their identify verified through Australia Post.

Given that Standards are used for buying and selling property, it makes sense that they are tough. That said, with the prevalence of identify fraud these days, it would be prudent to apply the same high standards when you want to confirm someone's identity.

How to identify another business

Now it is time to put everything you have learnt into practice by following these three steps to properly identify another business.

Reverse engineering

To help understand the different entities and structures, we started with individuals (sole traders), then partnerships, companies, trusts and finally combination structures.

To identify a business, it is best to work in reverse. This is because when dealing with another business, what we are usually presented with is the highest level of the structure, like the old tip of an iceberg analogy.

But it is not enough to stop at the tip because, as you should have picked up in the previous section, if you are going to have any chance enforcing a contract or pursuing a debt, you need to look below the top layer to find out what assets are potentially exposed or who can be held responsible.

After you read through this section, for each business you deal with, you should test out the following hypothetical.

A trip to your lawyer

Imagine the other business has defaulted on your agreement and you now need to sue them for damages. You are sitting in your lawyer's office where you are asked the following questions:

1. Which entity are you going to sue?
2. Does that entity have assets you can pursue?
3. Is there an individual you could also sue?

For each of these questions, you should have evidence to support your answers, such as a written contract with the entity you are going to sue, a security interest over an asset, or a personal guarantee provided by the person you are suing.

This exercise may prove disconcerting for some business owners as they realise how tenuous some of their key business relationships may be.

Step 1 Core information

The first thing you should do is request the following information from the other business:

ABN*	
Registered business name (*if they have one*)	
Are they using a trust structure?	Yes / No
Name of trust	
Name of trustee	
Are they using a company?	Yes / No
Company's ACN	
Are they using a partnership?	Yes / No
Name partners	

* If the other business is hesitant in providing an active ABN, this should be cause for concern (see earlier discussion on the importance of ABNs).

Step 2 Searches

With the above information, you should conduct the following searches:

ABN search

- Australian Government's Australian Business Register – ABN Lookup: https://abr.business.gov.au/ (this is a free search)

Business name search (if they have a registered business name)

- Business Name Register at ASIC Connect: https://asic.gov.au/online-services/search-asics-registers/business-names/ (this is a free search)

ACN search (if using a company)

- ASIC Connect: https://connectonline.asic.gov.au/ (this is a paid search)
- Go do -> Search ASIC Registers -> Search within: Organisation & Business Names
- Under 'Company extract' order 'Current company information'

Step 3 Complete details

You should now be able to complete the following information (*where applicable*):

Trust

Trust name	
Trustee name	
Trustee entity type	
For the trustee, complete the table for the applicable entity type (ie. if an individual, complete the Individuals table; and if a company, complete the Company table)	

Company

ACN	
Company name	
Registered business name of company (*if applicable*)	
Registered address	
Principle place of business	
Phone number of company	
Email of company	
Names of each director	
For each director, complete the table for Individuals	

Partnerships

Name of partnership	
Registered business name of partnership (*if applicable*)	
Registered address of partnership	
Names and entity type of each partner	
For each partner, complete the table for the applicable entity type (ie. if an individual, complete the Individuals table; if a company, complete the Companies table)	

Individuals (including sole trader)

Name	
Registered address	
Personal address	
Phone number	
Email	
Verification of identity	Yes / No

References

[1] Partnership Act 1958 (Vic) s 8.
[2] Partnership Act 1958 (Vic) s 9.
[3] Partnership Act 1958 (Vic) s 9.
[4] Partnership Act 1958 (Vic) s 13.
[5] Partnership Act 1958 (Vic) s 14.
[6] Partnership Act 1958 (Vic) s 5.
[7] Partnership Act 1958 (Vic) s 8.
[8] Partnership Act 1958 (Vic) ss 24 to 28.
[9] Partnership Act 1958 (Vic) ss 36 to 45.
[10] Partnership Act 1958 (Vic) s 23.
[11] Graw, Stephen, *An Outline of the Law of Partnership*, Thomson Reuters (Professional) Australia Limited, 4th Edition 2011, p 195.
[12] *Australian Taxation Office* website - https://www.ato.gov.au/Business/Changing,-selling-or-closing-your-business/In-detail/Changing-the-makeup-of-a-partnership/
[13] Ibid.
[14] Partnership Act 1958 (Vic) s 41.
[15] Partnership Act 1958 (Vic) s 28(1).
[16] Partnership Act 1958 (Vic) s 23.
[17] Corporations Act 2001 (Cth) s 115.
[18] Corporations Act 2001 (Cth) s 119.
[19] Corporations Act 2001 (Cth) s 124.
[20] Lipton, Herzberg and Welsh, *Understanding Company Law,* Thomson Reuters (Professional) Australia Limited, p 37, paragraph 2.70.
[21] Corporations Act 2001 (Cth) s 181.
[22] Corporations Act 2001 (Cth) s 9.
[23] Corporations Act 2001 (Cth) s 198A.
[24] Corporations Act 2001 (Cth) s 127.
[25] Corporations Act 2001 (Cth) s 198C.
[26] Corporations Act 2001 (Cth) s 126.
[27] Corporations Act 2001 (Cth) s 201G.

[28] Corporations Act 2001 (Cth) s 203C.
[29] Corporations Act 2001 (Cth) s 202A.
[30] Corporations Act 2001 (Cth) s 248 (directors' meetings) s 249 (members' meetings).
[31] Corporations Act 2001 (Cth) s 135.
[32] Corporations Act 2001 (Cth) s 140.
[33] Corporations Act 2001 (Cth) ss 180 to 184.
[34] Fair Work Act 2009 (Cth) s 550.
[35] Occupational Health and Safety Act 2004 (Vic) s 144.
[36] Taxation Administration Act 1953 (Cth), Schedule 1, s 269-5.
[37] Environment Protection Act 1970 (Vic) s 66B.
[38] Competition and Consumer Act 2010 (Cth) s 76.
[39] Corporations Act 2001 (Cth) s 588G.
[40] Corporations Act 2001 (Cth) s 9.
[41] Corporations Act 2001 (Cth) s 588G.
[42] Corporations Act 2001 (Cth) s 588G(3).
[43] Corporations Act 2001 (Cth) s 95A(1).
[44] ASIC Regulatory Guide 217 - Duty to prevent insolvent trading: Guide for directors, 29 July 2010.
[45] Corporations Act 2001 (Cth) s 588E.
[46] *Corporations Act 2001* (Cth) ss 232 to 235.
[47] Corporations Act 2001 (Cth) ss 233.
[48] Corporations Act 2001 (Cth) s 114.
[49] Corporations Act 2001 (Cth) s 201A(1).
[50] Corporations Act 2001 (Cth) s 201D.
[51] Corporations Act 2001 (Cth) s 114(1).
[52] Corporations Act 2001 (Cth) s 153(1).
[53] Corporations Act 2001 (Cth) s 153(2).
[54] Corporations Act 2001 (Cth) s 1072A.
[55] Corporations Act 2001 (Cth) s 601AA.
[56] Corporations Act 2001 (Cth) s 601AB.
[57] Corporations Act 2001 (Cth) s 601AH.
[58] Income Tax Rates Act 1986 (Cth) s 23.
[59] Trustee Act 1958 (Vic) s 36(2).
[60] Agardy, Peter, *Trading Trusts Explained*, LexisNexis 2018, Para 14.2.
[61] Trustee Act 1958 (Vic) s 2(3).

[62] *State Revenue Office of Victoria* website - https://www.sro.vic.gov.au/land-transfer-duty-current-rates
[63] Agardy, Peter, *Trading Trusts Explained*, LexisNexis 2018, Para 19.2.
[64] Perpetuities and Accumulations Act 1968 (Vic) s 5.
[65] Income Tax Assessment Act 1936 (Cth) s 97 and s 101.
[66] Income Tax Assessment Act 1936 (Cth) s 99A.
[67] Income Tax Assessment Act 1997 (Cth) s 115.100.
[68] Land Tax Act 2005 (Vic) Schedule 1.
[69] *Australian Taxation Office* website - https://www.ato.gov.au/Individuals/Investing/In-detail/Children-and-under-18s/Your-income-if-you-are-under-18-years-old/?page=3#Higher_tax_rates
[70] Income Tax Assessment Act 1936 (Cth) s 102AG.
[71] Latimer, Paul, *Australian Business Law,* Oxford University Press, 35th Edition 2016, p 664, paragraph 9-140.
[72] Franchising Code of Conduct s 2(3).
[73] Competition and Consumer (Industry Codes—Franchising) Regulation 2014 (Cth).
[74] A New Tax System (Australian Business Number) Act 1999 (Cth) s 3(2).
[75] Business Names Registration Act 2011 (Cth) s 18.
[76] Taxation Administration Act 1953 (Cth), Schedule 1, s 12-190.
[77] A New Tax System (Australian Business Number) Act 1999 (Cth) s 23.
[78] Business Names Registration Act 2011 (Cth) s 19(1).
[79] Business Names Registration Act 2011 (Cth) s 20(1).
[80] Business Names Registration Act 2011 (Cth) s 18(2).
[81] Business Names Registration Act 2011 (Cth) s 18(1).
[82] Business Names Registration Act 2011 (Cth) s 17.
[83] Corporations Act 2001 (Cth) s 114(1).
[84] Corporations Act 2001 (Cth) s 153(1).
[85] Corporations Act 2001 (Cth) s 153(2).

[86] Australian Registrars' National Electronic Conveyancing Council (ARNECC) Model Participation Rules Version 5, 21 December 2018.
[87] Ibid s 2.
[88] Ibid s. 3.
[89] Ibid s 3 - Minimum Document Requirements.

www.ingramcontent.com/pod-product-compliance
Lightning Source LLC
Chambersburg PA
CBHW050012230526
45465CB00003BB/1391